SCHOLASTI

Lift-the-Flap
Alphabet

Instant Manipulatives That Teach Each Letter of the Alphabet

Betty Jo Evers

New York • Toronto • London • Auckland • Sydney
Mexico City • New Delhi • Hong Kong • Buenos Aires

Teaching *Resources*

Dedication

To David, my husband and friend,
for encouraging me to believe in myself.

Acknowledgements

To Frank Davidson, Superintendent of Schools in Casa Grande Elementary School District,
and Norm Sam, Principal in Casa Grande Elementary School District:
Thank you for your leadership, guidance, and respect.

Thank you to the teachers in my life for their friendship, kind words, and support.

- -

Edited by Immacula A. Rhodes
Cover design by Maria Lilja
Interior design by Holly Grundon

ISBN: 978-0-545-28077-8

Lift-the-Flap Manipulatives

About This Book

Welcome to *Lift-the-Flap Alphabet*! The manipulatives and interactive activities in this book are designed to give children practice in recognizing letters and their sounds. Research shows that phonemic awareness—the ability to hear and manipulate sounds in oral language—and phonics (attaching letter sounds to their printed symbols) are both crucial to a child's development of reading skills. In *What Research Has to Say About Fluency Instruction* (2006), S. J. Samuels and A. E. Farstrup state, "The ability to hear and manipulate sounds in spoken words strongly predicts the future success in learning to read. Fluency in letter recognition and sound association should be effortless and automatic. It is the foundation of word recognition." Children must have both phonemic awareness and an understanding of phonics to become successful readers and writers.

The pictures in these reproducible, easy-to-assemble manipulatives offer children multiple opportunities to practice saying words that begin with each letter of the alphabet, identifying those sounds, and matching them to their corresponding letters. (Note that for the letter *X*, the manipulatives feature words that *end* with that letter sound.) The playful format is a fun and inviting way to teach letter-sound associations and reinforce children's learning. Donald Bear, in *Words Their Way* (2000), notes that children can learn these associations at the same time they are learning to reflect on their oral language. In addition to learning letters, the pictures in the activities can be used to help extend vocabulary, increase comprehension, and reinforce speaking in complete, fluent sentences. According to research, oral language development is critical for comprehension. When a child discusses what he or she already knows about a picture, his or her prior knowledge has been activated, and the child is focused and ready to learn more about that topic. Using these activities to reinforce and enrich children's letter-sound knowledge and vocabulary development allows you to address the five components identified by the National Reading Panel for successful reading: phonemic awareness, phonics, vocabulary, comprehension, and fluency.

You can use the lift-the-flap manipulatives and activities for direct, one-on-one or small-group instruction, place the manipulatives in a center for children to use independently or in pairs, or send them home for extra practice. The flexibility of the activities allows you to use them in any order and any way that best suits your students' needs for individualization and differentiation. A reproducible assessment form is also provided to help you record and monitor each child's progress throughout the year.

References

Bear, D. (2000). *Words their way*. Columbus, OH: Merrill.

Samuels, S. Jay & A. E. Farstrup, editors. (2006). *What research has to say about fluency instruction*. Newark, DE: IRA.

National Reading Panel (2000). *Teaching children to read: An evidence-based assessment of the scientific research literature on reading and its implications for reading instruction*. Washington, DC: National Institute of Child Health and Development.

Preparing the Lift-the-Flap Manipulatives

The lift-the-flap manipulatives are easy to assemble and use. Just follow these simple directions and the manipulatives are ready to go!

What You Need

* lift-the-flap patterns for the selected letter

* letter cards (pages 46–47)

* colored markers

* scissors

* craft glue (or strong, clear tape)

What to Do

1. Cut out the lift-the-flap patterns and letter cards.

2. If desired, color the pictures on the large pattern.

3. Laminate the patterns and cards.

4. Glue (or tape) the question-mark flap to the center of the large pattern where indicated.

Using the Lift-the-Flap Manipulatives

Demonstrate how to use the lift-the-flap manipulatives to do the activity, then invite children to complete each activity independently or with a partner.

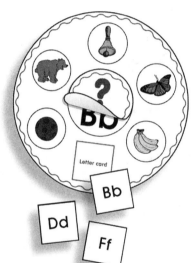

1. Spread the letter cards faceup on a table.

2. Name one picture at a time on the lift-the-flap manipulative.

3. Think about the sound at the beginning of each word. What letter makes that sound?

4. Find the matching letter card. Place it on the box below the flap.

5. Lift the flap to check your answer.

Using the Assessment Form

Copy the assessment form (page 7) and use it with the lift-the-flap manipulatives and letter cards to record and monitor children's progress. You might prepare separate letter cards for each uppercase and lowercase letter to use for assessment.

To use, show the child a lift-the-flap manipulative. Point to a picture and ask the child to name it. Have the child say the first sound in that word. If correct, check the corresponding box on the form. Next, ask the child to name the letter that makes that sound and then find the uppercase and/or lowercase letter card for the sound. Each time, record the child's response on the form, if correct.

Activities to Extend Learning

Use these activities to give children additional opportunities to explore and practice letter-sound skills.

* Encourage children to practice writing the letter from the activity. As they write, ask them to voice the letter sound. They might also draw pictures for other words that begin with that letter sound.

* Have children search magazines, sales flyers, and catalogs for pictures that begin with a letter sound of their choice. Invite them to cut out the pictures to create a collage.

* Invite student pairs to name and share what they know about each picture on a lift-the-flap manipulative. Then have them identify the beginning sound of the picture names and tell what letter makes that sound.

* Challenge children to alphabetize the lift-the-flap manipulatives (use one for each letter). Ask them to name the letter and letter sound represented by each manipulative.

* Spread the manipulatives facedown on a table. Invite children to take turns picking a manipulative, naming the pictures on it, and identifying the letter for the beginning sound. If correct, the child keeps the manipulative. If not, the child returns it to the table. Continue until all the manipulatives have been claimed.

Meeting the Language Arts Standards

The activities in this book are designed to support you in meeting the national and state language arts standards.

Connections to the McREL Language Arts Standards

Mid-continent Research for Education and Learning (McREL), a nationally recognized nonprofit organization, has compiled and evaluated national and state standards—and proposed what teachers should provide for their PreK–1 students to grow proficient in language arts. This book's activities support the following standards:

Uses general skill and strategies of the reading process including:
* Knows uppercase and lowercase letters of the alphabet
* Uses basic elements of phonetic analysis (e.g., understands sound-symbol relationships; beginning and ending consonants; vowel sounds)

Uses grammatical and mechanical conventions in written compositions including:
* Uses conventions of print in writing (e.g., forms letters in print, uses uppercase and lowercase letters of the alphabet)

Source: Kendall, J. S. & Marzano, R. J. (2004). *Content knowledge: A compendium of standards and benchmarks for K–12 education.* Aurora, CO: Mid-continent Research for Education and Learning. Online database: http://www.mcrel.org/standards-benchmarks/

Connections to Early Childhood Language Arts Standards

The activities in this book are also designed to support you in meeting the following PreK–1 literacy goals and recommendations established in a joint position statement by the International Reading Association (IRA) and the National Association for the Education of Young Children (NAEYC):

* Understands that print carries a message
* Engages in reading and writing attempts
* Recognizes letters and letter-sound matches
* Begins to write

Source: *Learning to Read and Write: Developmentally Appropriate Practices for Young Children*, a joint position statement of the International Reading Association (IRA) and the National Association for the Education of Young Children (NAEYC).
http://www.naeyc.org/about/positions/pdf/PSPREAD98.PDF
© 1998 by the National Association for the Education of Young Children

Common Core State Standards

The activities in this book also correlate with the English Language Arts standards recommended by the Common Core State Standards Initiative, a state-led effort to establish a single set of clear educational standards whose aim is to provide students with a high-quality education. At the time this book went to press, these standards were still being finalized. To learn more, go to www.corestandards.org.

Assessment Form

Name _____   Teacher _____

Directions

Point to a picture. Ask the child to name the picture then:

1. Say its beginning sound.
2. Name the letter for that sound.
3. Find the letter card for that sound.

Letter	Says the Sound	Names the Letter	Chooses the Letter Card
A			
B			
C			
D			
E			
F			
G			
H			
I			
J			
K			
L			
M			
N			
O			
P			
Q			
R			
S			
T			
U			
V			
W			
X			
Y			
Z			

Letter	Says the Sound	Names the Letter	Chooses the Letter Card
a			
b			
c			
d			
e			
f			
g			
h			
i			
j			
k			
l			
m			
n			
o			
p			
q			
r			
s			
t			
u			
v			
w			
x			
y			
z			

Glue flap here.

Aa

Letter card

?

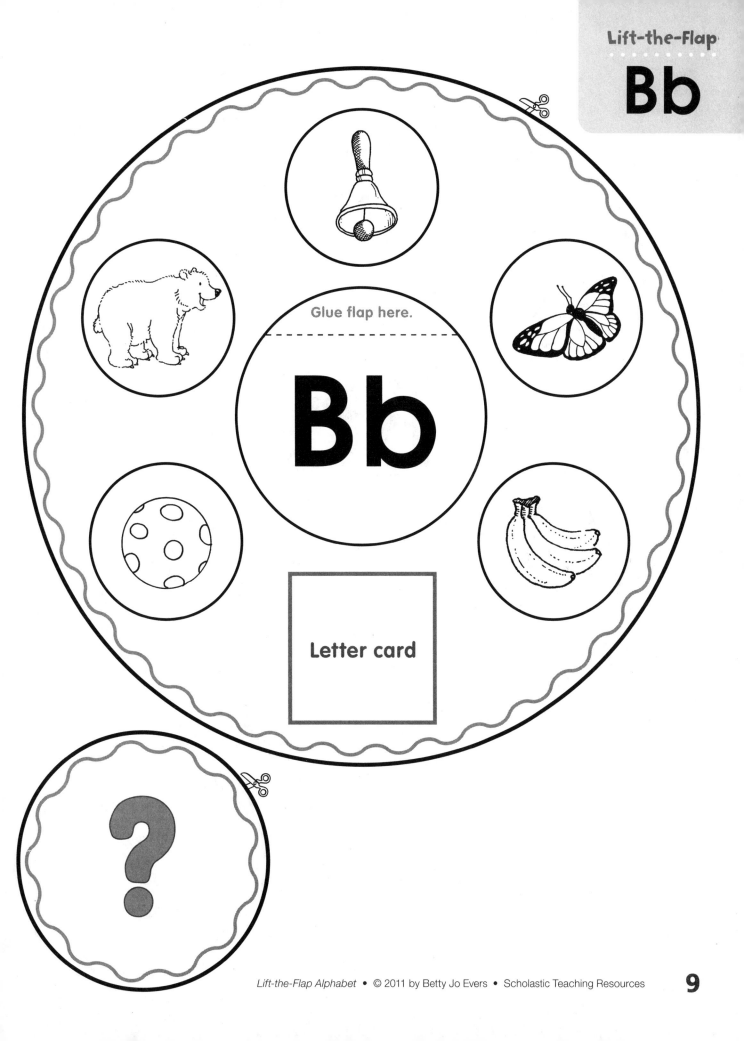

Glue flap here.

Bb

Letter card

?

Glue flap here.

Bb

Letter card

?

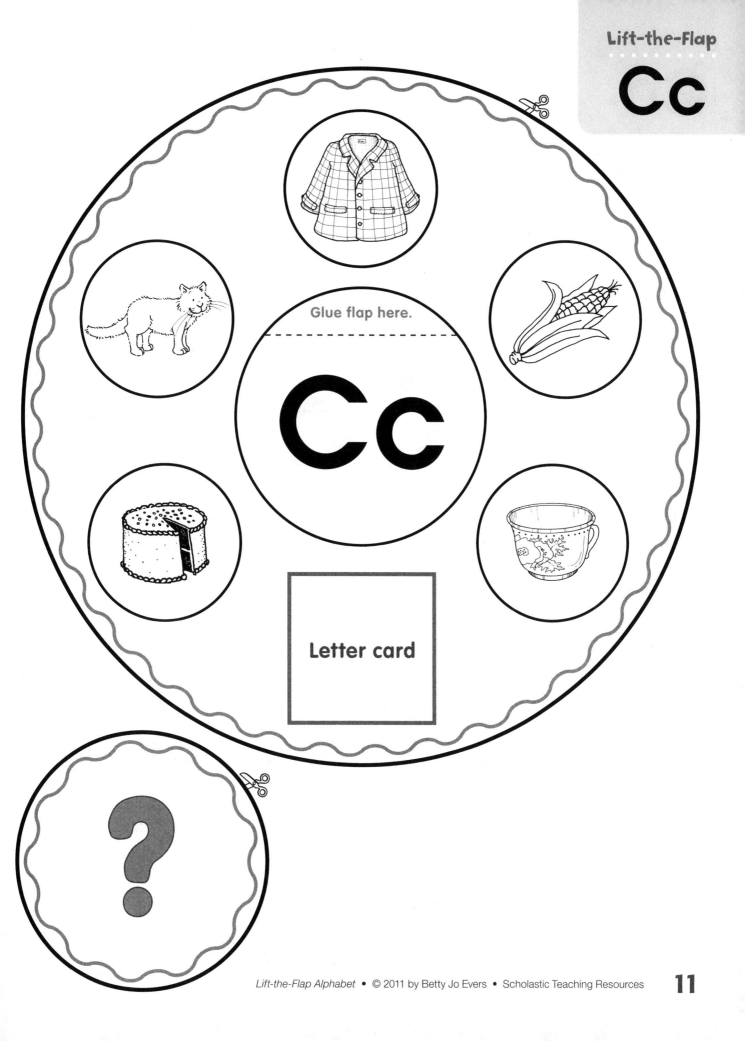

Glue flap here.

Cc

Letter card

?

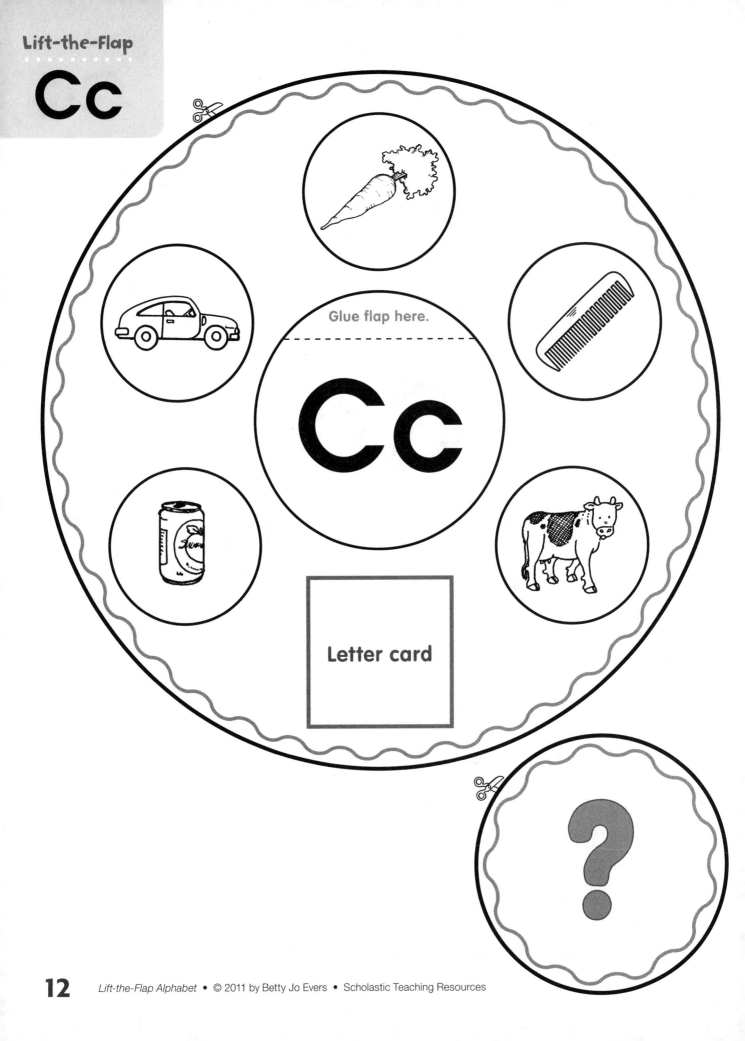

Glue flap here.

Cc

Letter card

?

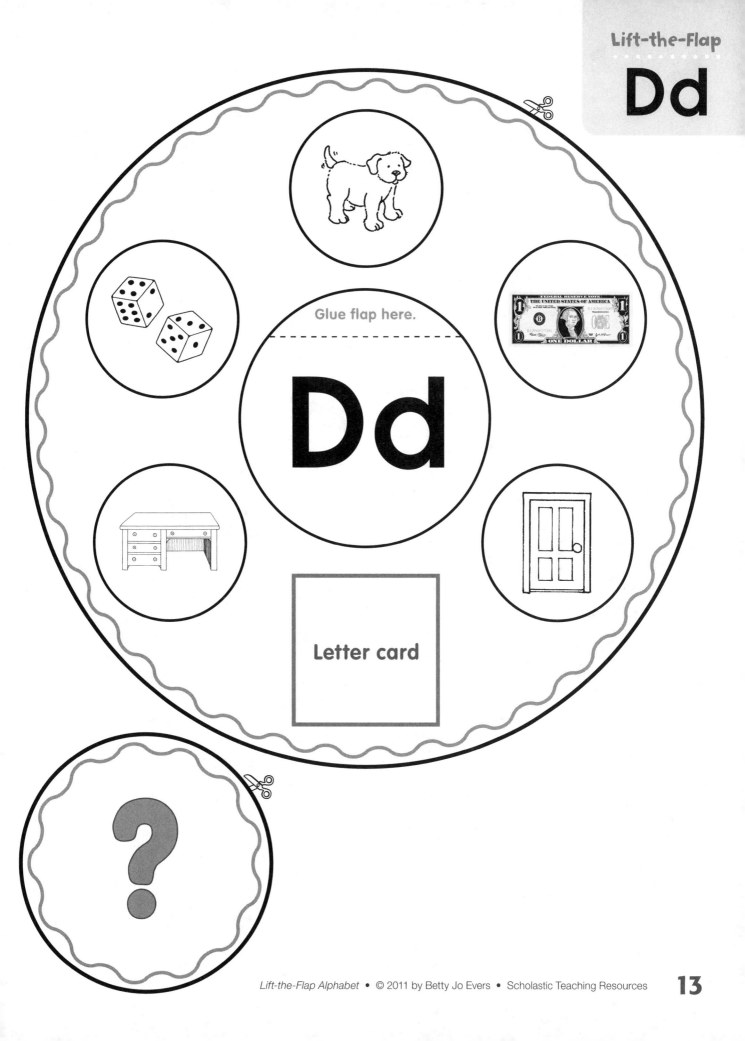

Glue flap here.

Dd

Letter card

?

Glue flap here.

Dd

Letter card

?

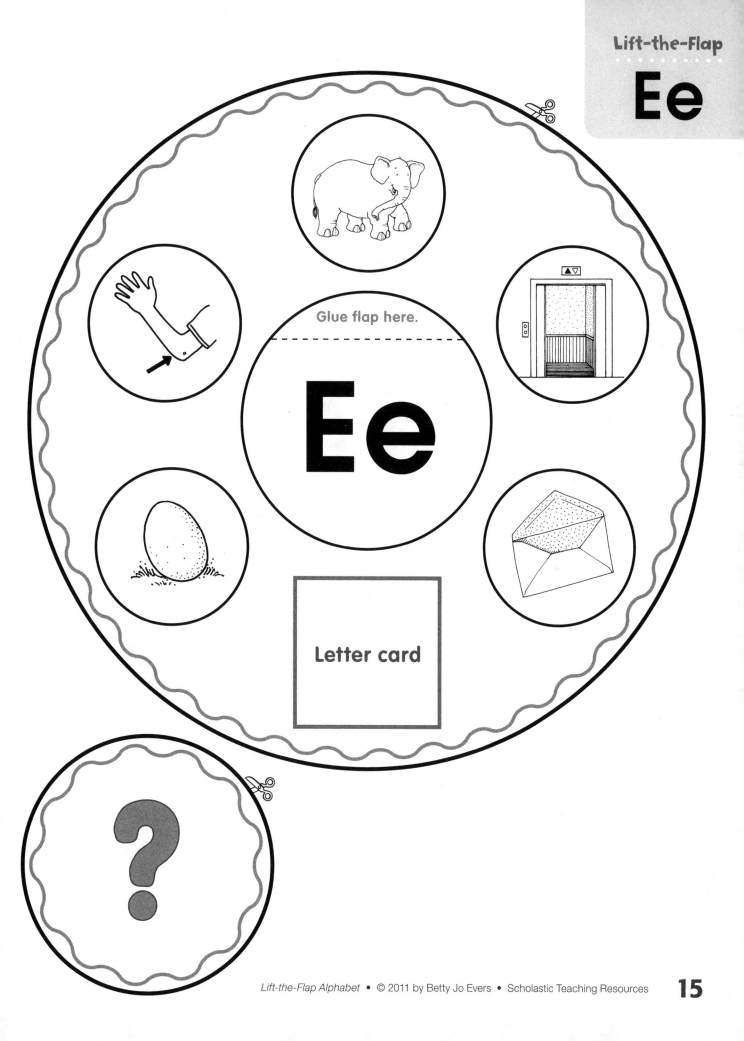

Glue flap here.

Ee

Letter card

Glue flap here.

Ff

Letter card

?

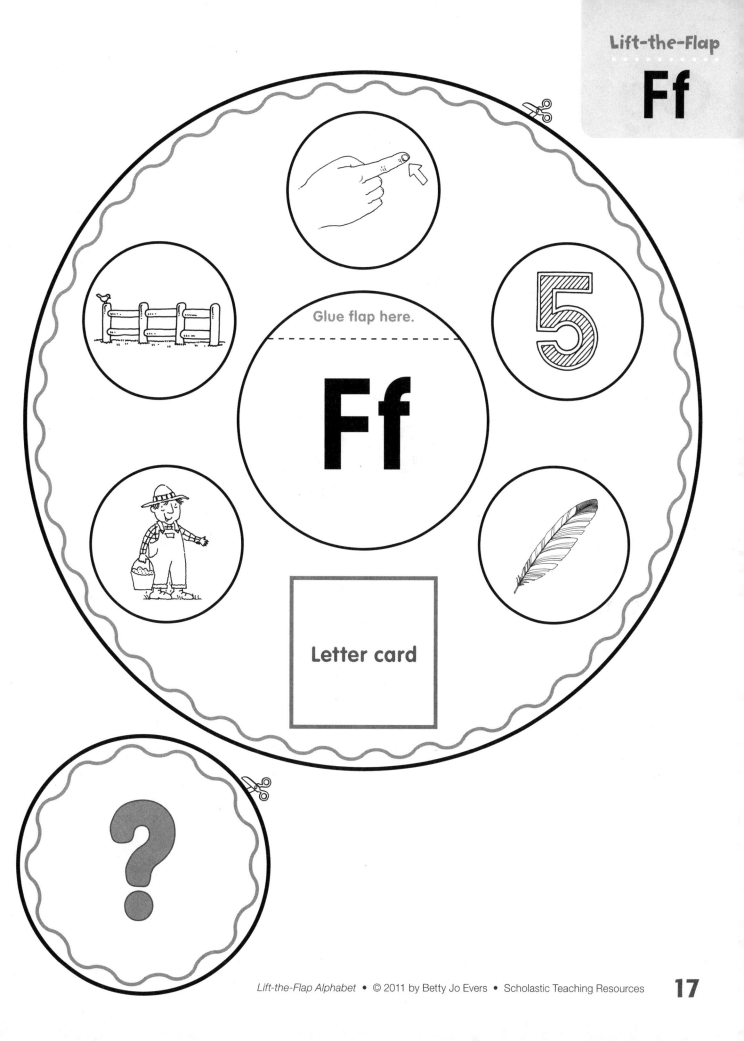

Glue flap here.

Ff

Letter card

Glue flap here.

Gg

Letter card

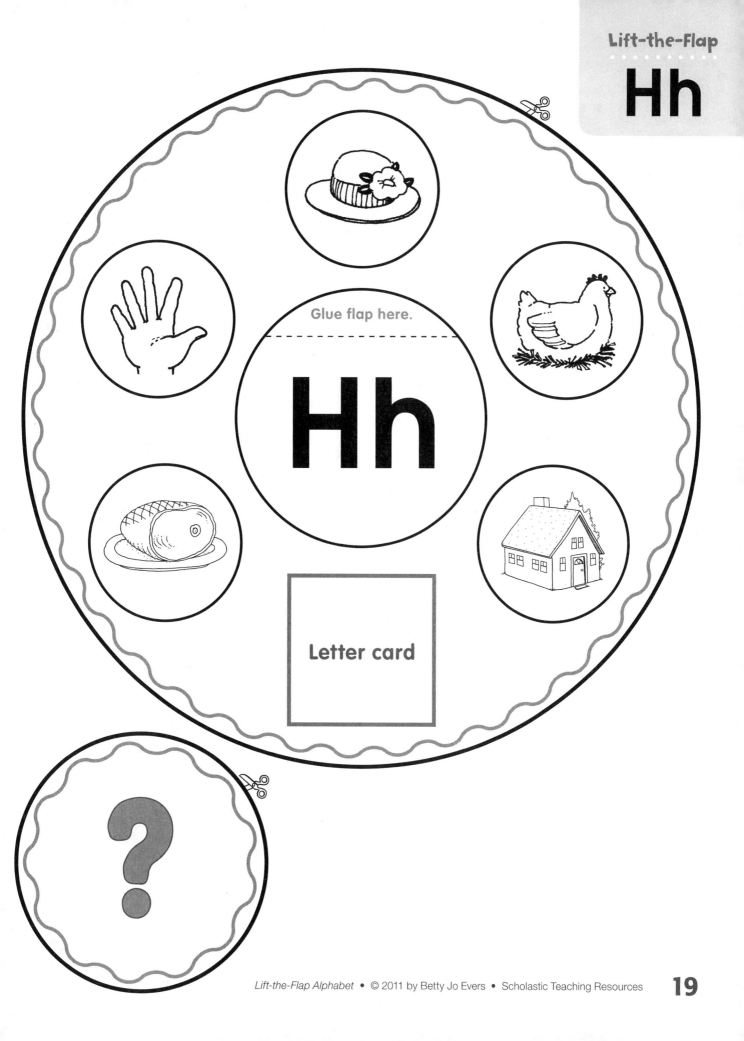

Glue flap here.

Hh

Letter card

?

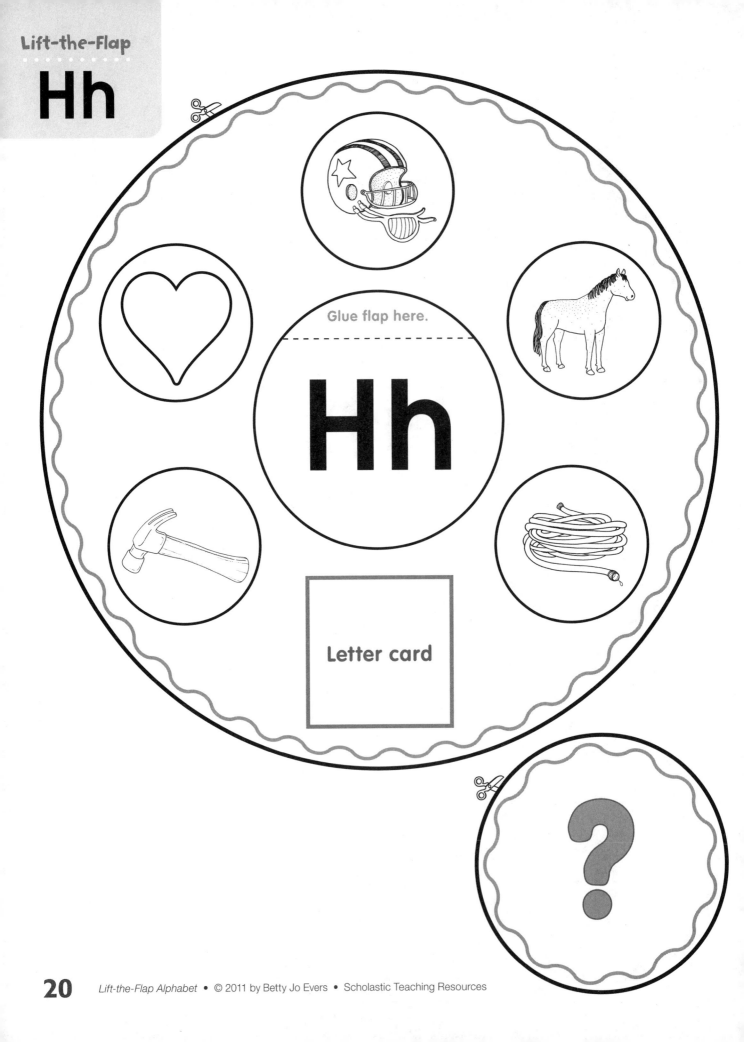

Glue flap here.

Hh

Letter card

?

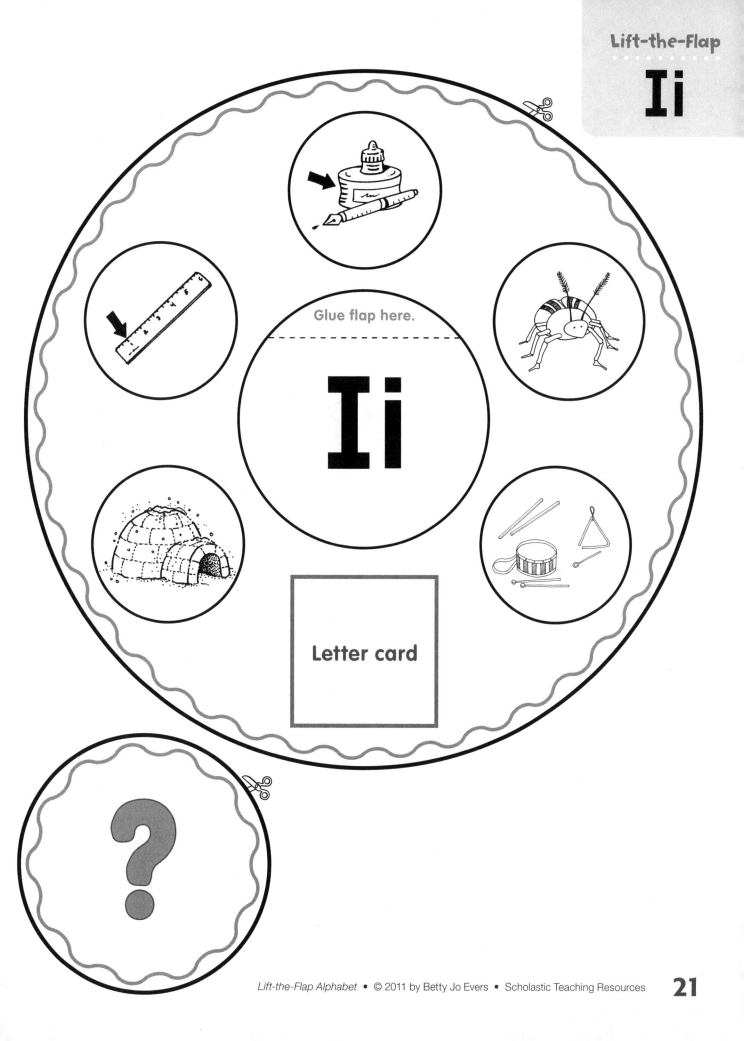

Glue flap here.

Ii

Letter card

?

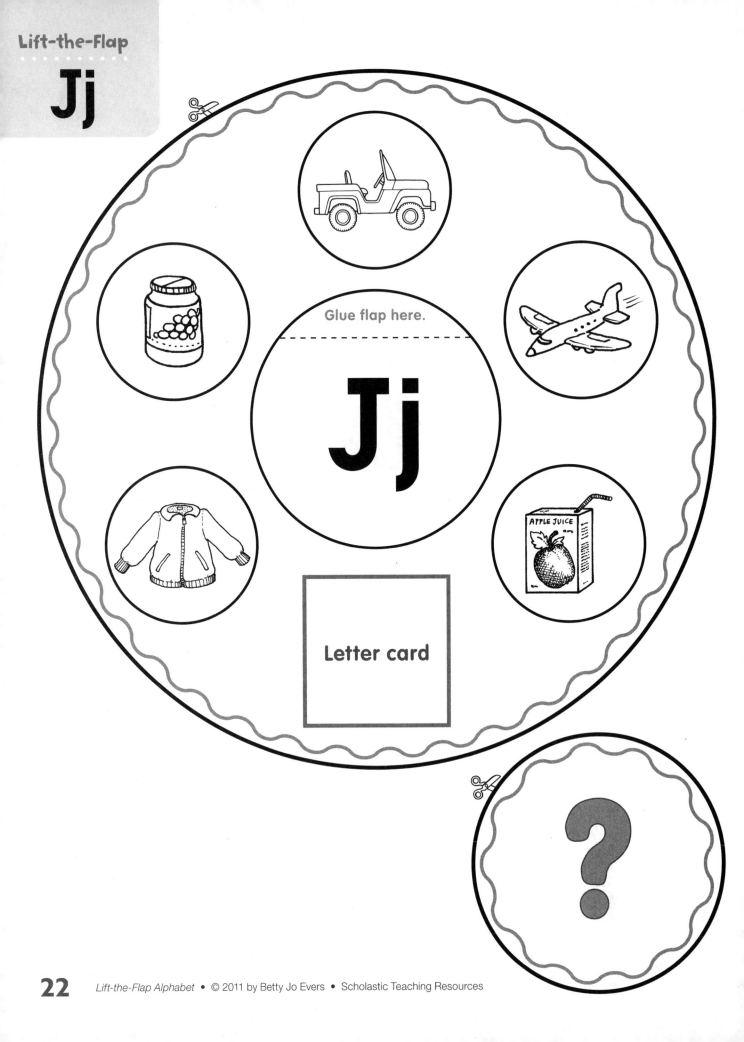

Glue flap here.

Jj

Letter card

?

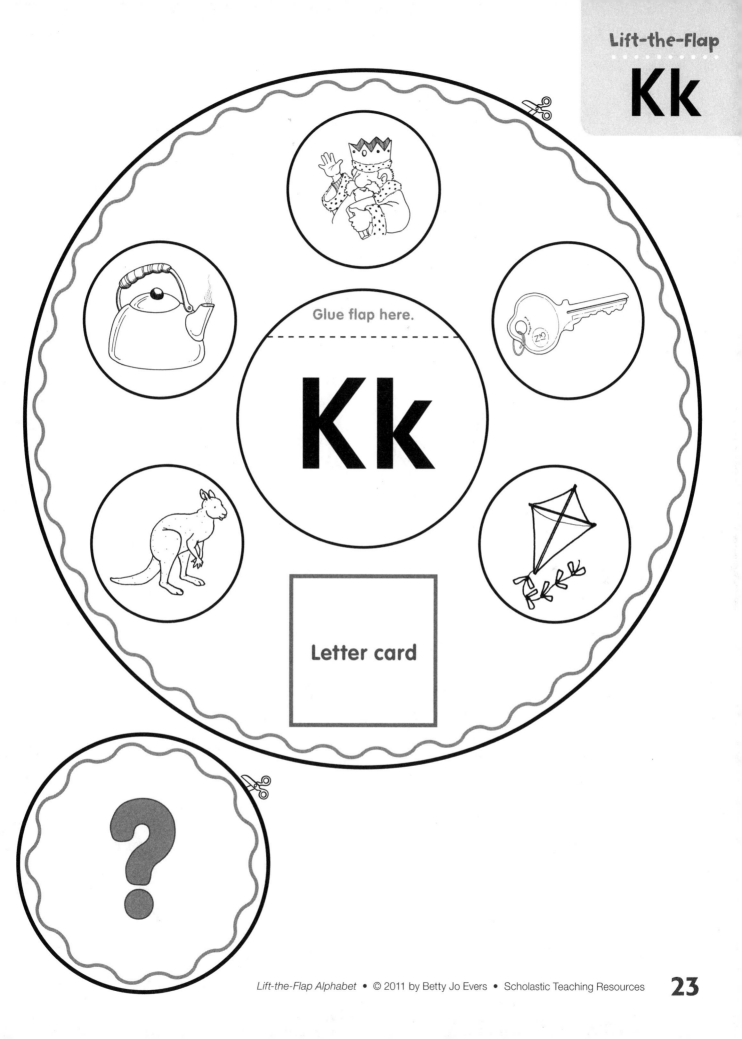

Glue flap here.

Kk

Letter card

?

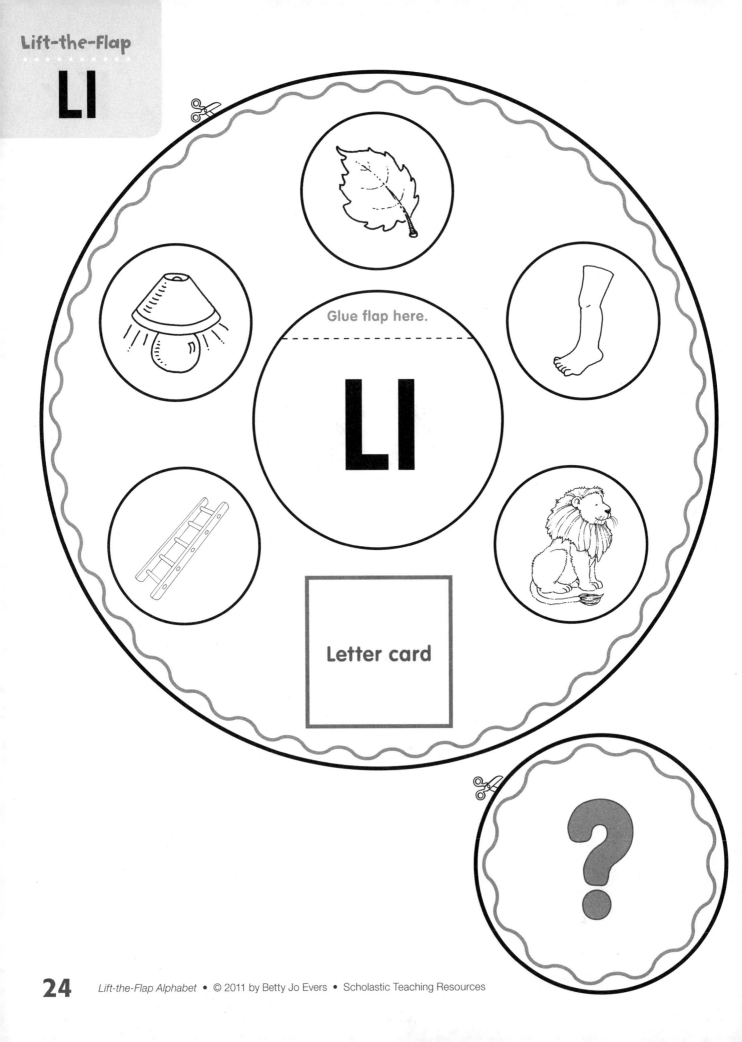

Glue flap here.

Ll

Letter card

?

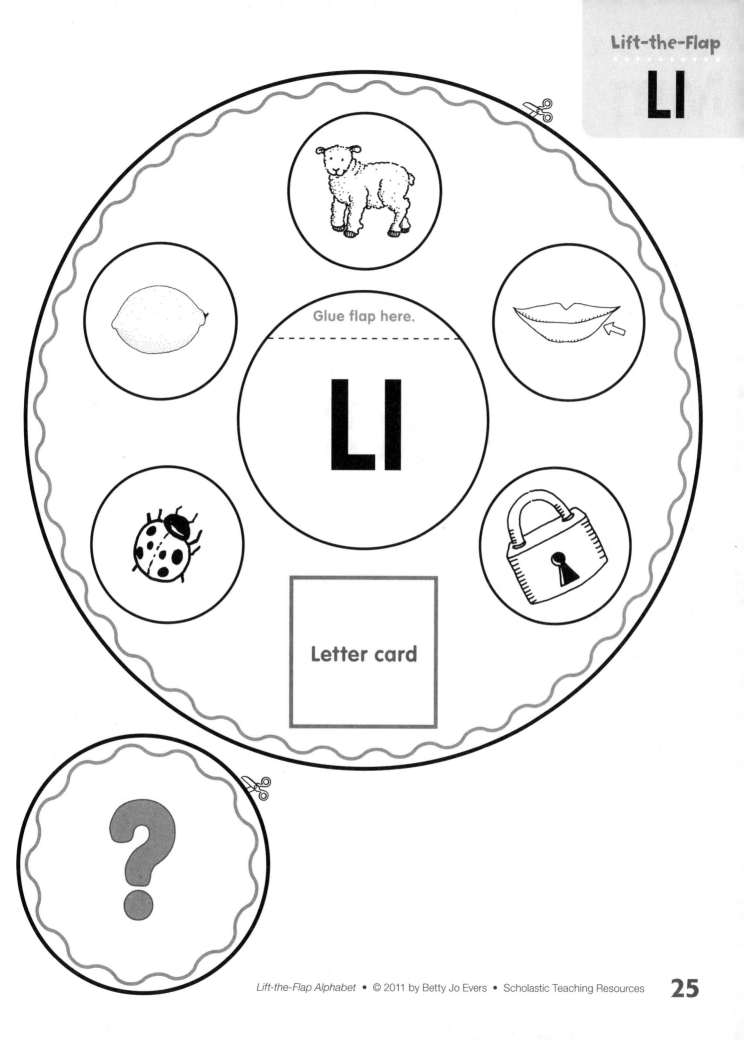

Glue flap here.

LI

Letter card

Glue flap here.

Mm

Letter card

?

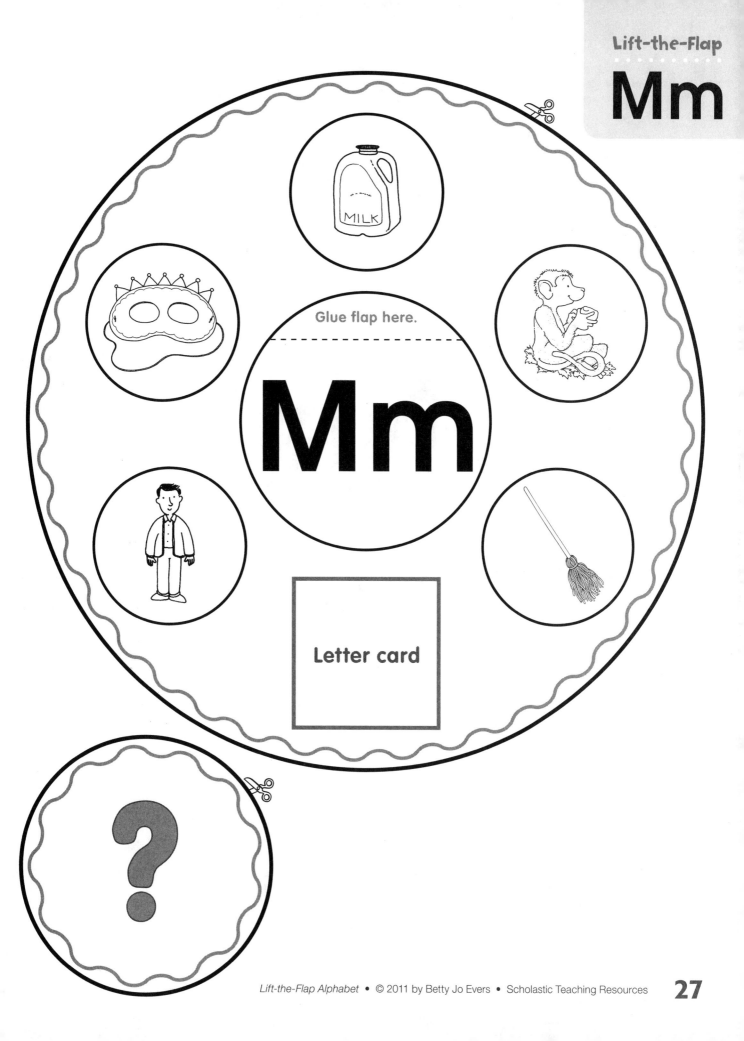

MILK

Glue flap here.

Mm

Letter card

?

Glue flap here.

Nn

Letter card

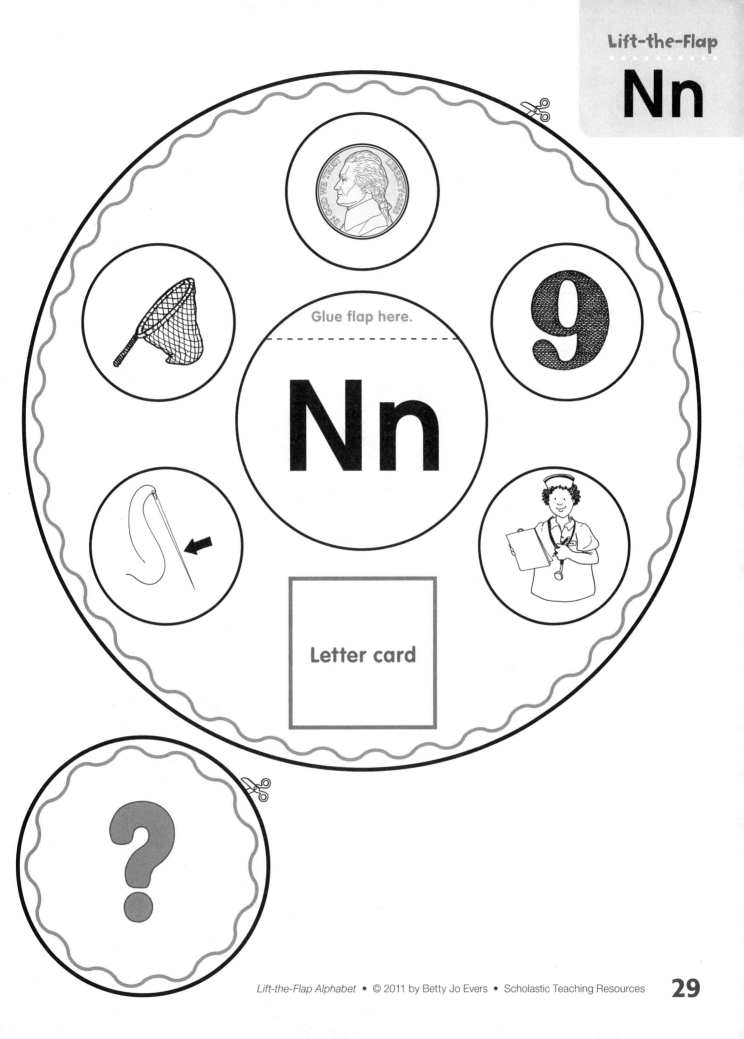

Glue flap here.

Nn

Letter card

?

Oo

Glue flap here.

Letter card

?

 Lift-the-Flap Alphabet • © 2011 by Betty Jo Evers • Scholastic Teaching Resources

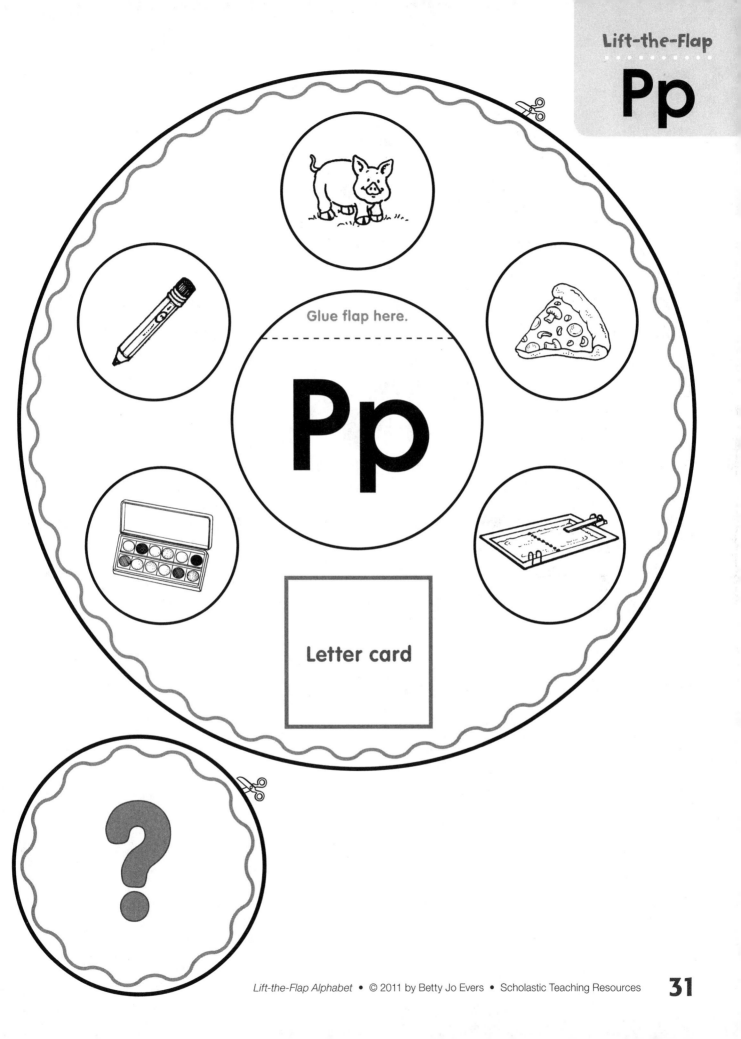

Glue flap here.

Pp

Letter card

?

Glue flap here.

Pp

Letter card

?

Glue flap here.

Qq

Letter card

Glue flap here.

Rr

Letter card

?

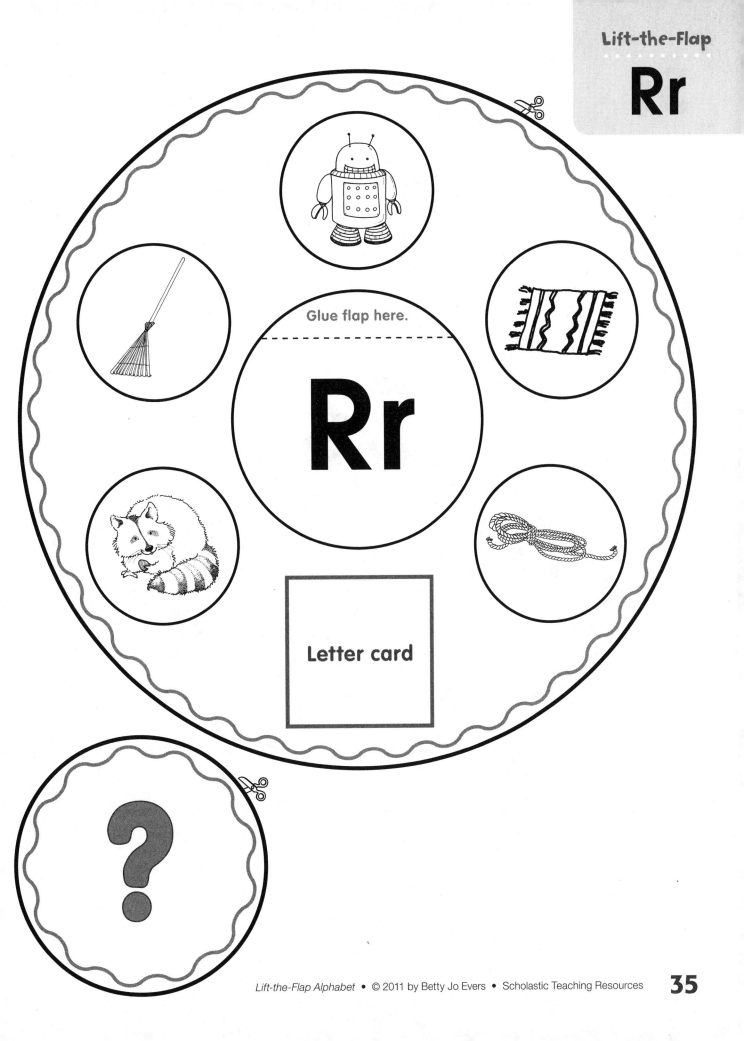

Glue flap here.

Rr

Letter card

?

Glue flap here.

Ss

Letter card

?

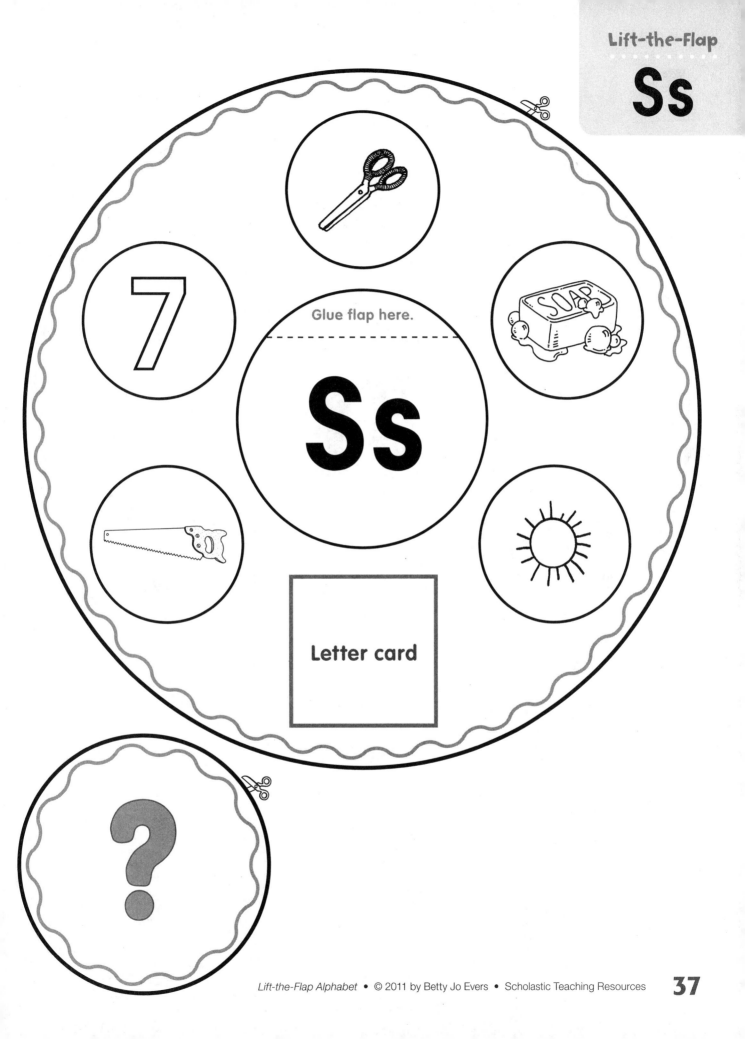

Glue flap here.

Ss

Letter card

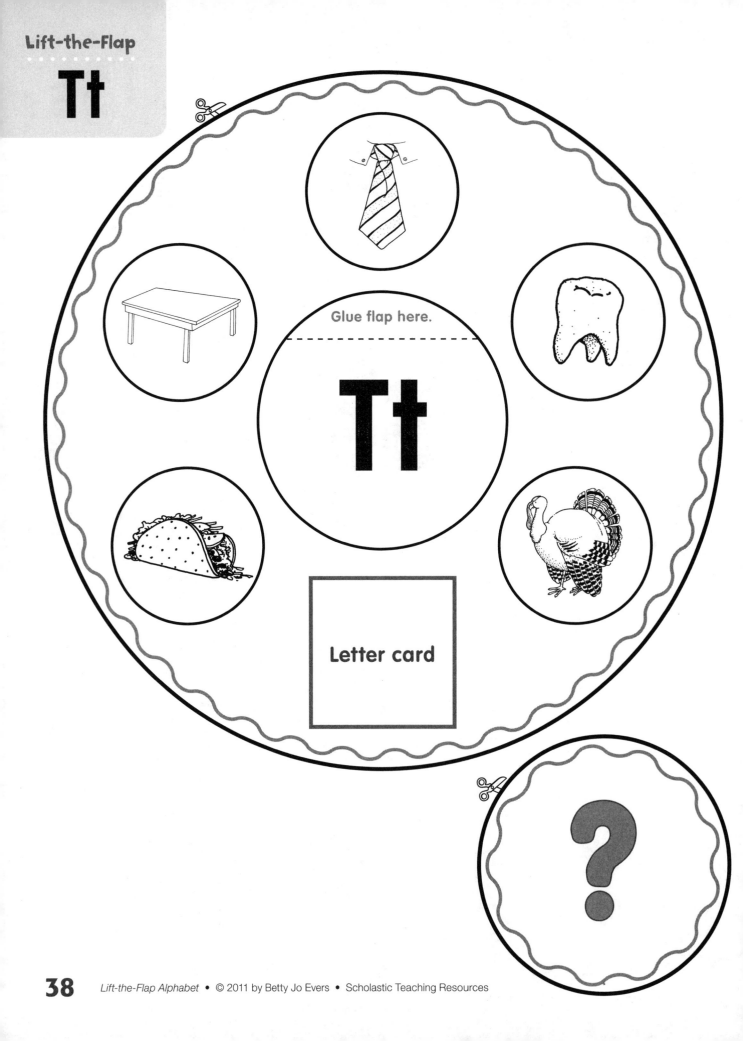

Glue flap here.

Tt

Letter card

?

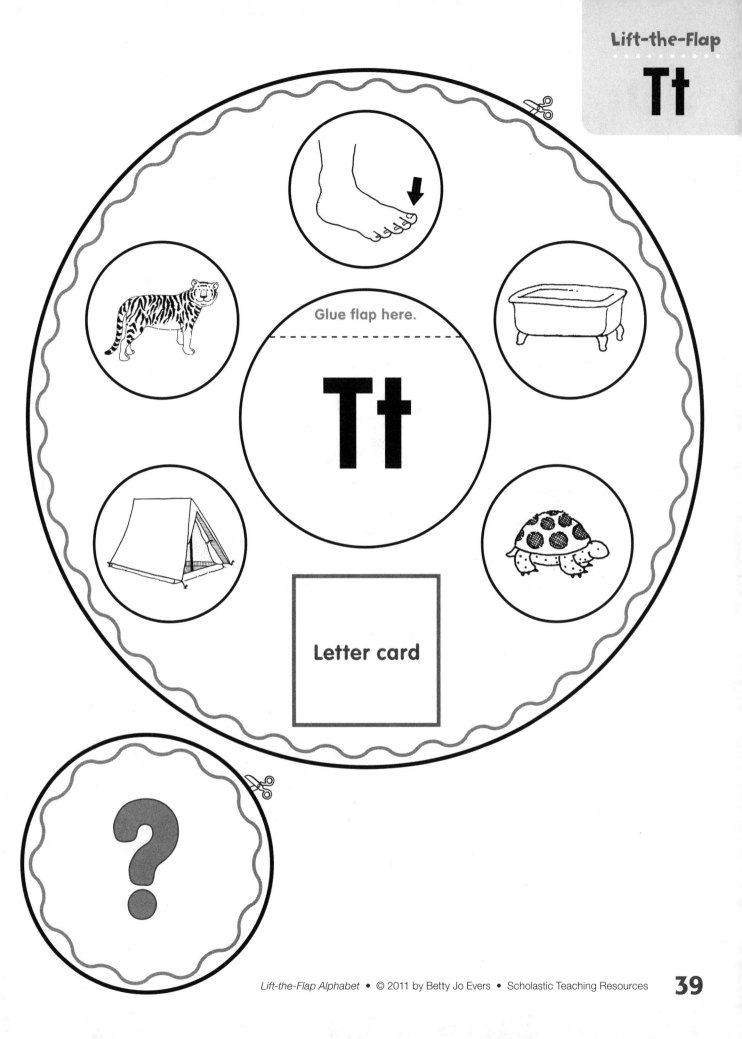

Lift-the-Flap

Tt

Glue flap here.

Tt

Letter card

?

Glue flap here.

Uu

Letter card

?

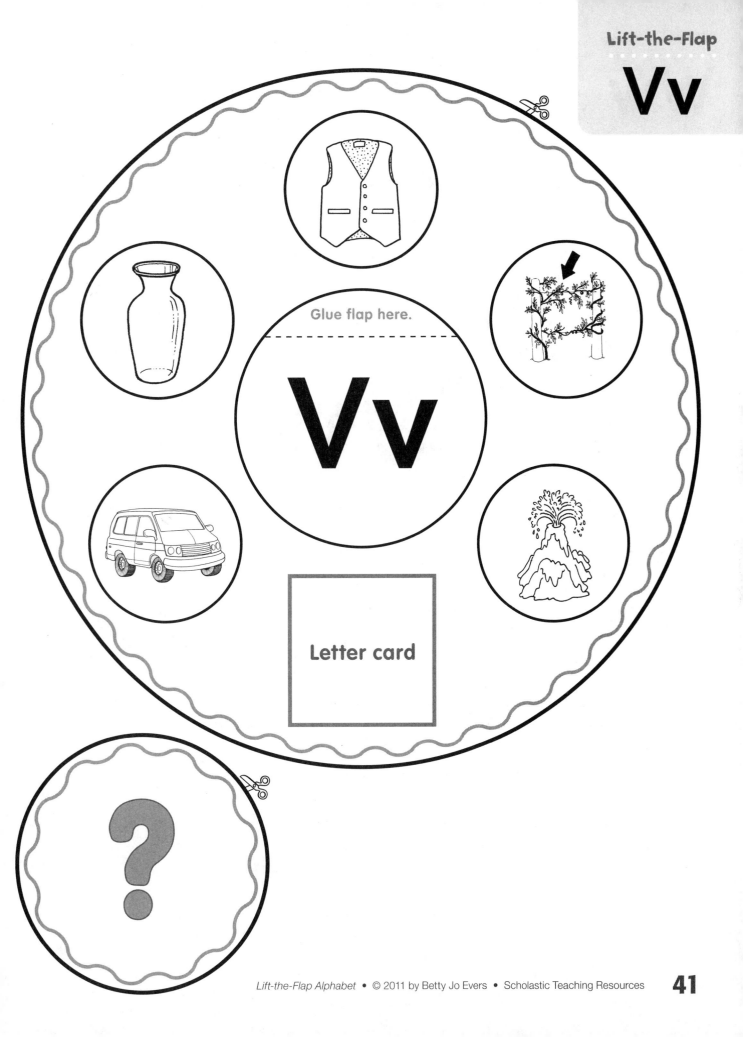

Glue flap here.

Vv

Letter card

Glue flap here.

Ww

Letter card

?

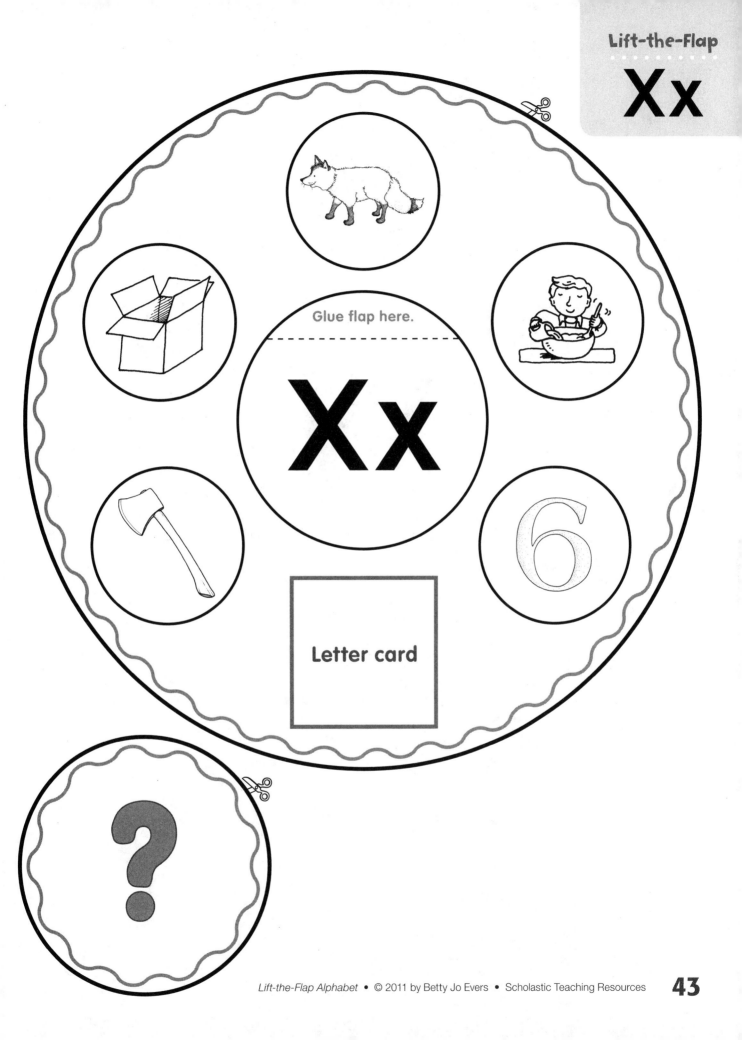

Glue flap here.

Xx

Letter card

?

Glue flap here.

Yy

Letter card

?

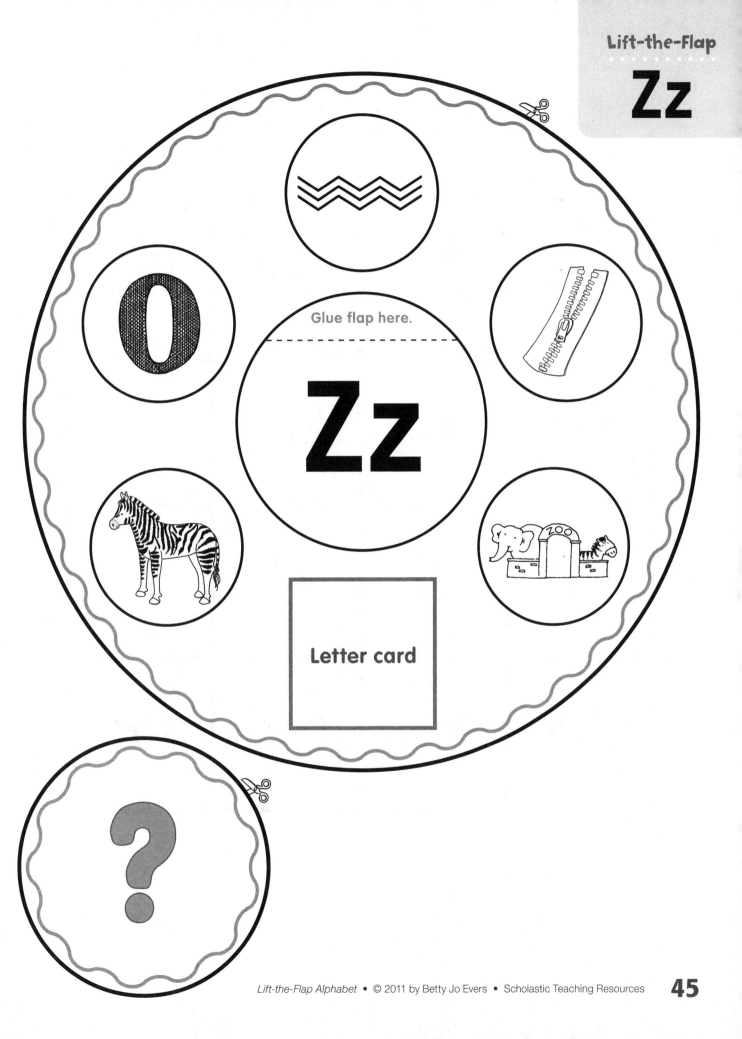

Glue flap here.

Zz

Letter card

Letter Cards

Aa	Bb	Cc	Dd
Ee	Ff	Gg	Hh
Ii	Jj	Kk	Ll
Mm	Nn	Oo	Pp

 Lift-the-Flap Alphabet • © 2011 by Betty Jo Evers • Scholastic Teaching Resources

Letter Cards

Qq	Rr	Ss	Tt
Uu	Vv	Ww	Xx
Yy	Zz		

Lift-the-Flap Word List

PAGE 8
Aa
ant
acrobat
apple
astronaut
alligator

PAGE 9
Bb
ball
bear
bell
butterfly
bananas

PAGE 10
Bb
balloon
bed
bee
bird
boat

PAGE 11
Cc
cake
cat
coat
corn
cup

PAGE 12
Cc
can
car
carrot
comb
cow

page 13
Dd
desk
dice
dog
dollar
door

PAGE 14
Dd
dart
deer
dime
doll
duck

PAGE 15
Ee
egg
elbow
elephant
elevator
envelope

PAGE 16
Ff
fan
foot
fire
fish
fork

PAGE 17
Ff
farmer
fence
finger
five
feather

PAGE 18
Gg
gate
gift
girl
goat
gum

PAGE 19
Hh
ham
hand
hat
hen
house

PAGE 20
Hh
hammer
heart
helmet
horse
hose

PAGE 21
Ii
igloo
inch
ink
insect
instruments

PAGE 22
Jj
jacket
jam
jeep
jet
juice

PAGE 23
Kk
kangaroo
kettle
king
key
kite

PAGE 24
Ll
ladder
lamp
leaf
leg
lion

PAGE 25
Ll
ladybug
lemon
lamb
lips
lock

PAGE 26
Mm
mat
mitten
moon
mouse
mug

PAGE 27
Mm
man
mask
milk
monkey
mop

PAGE 28
Nn
nail
neck
nest
nose
nut

PAGE 29
Nn
needle
net
nickel
nine
nurse

PAGE 30
Oo
octopus
olive
ostrich
otter
owl

PAGE 31
Pp
paint
pencil
pig
pizza
pool

PAGE 32
Pp
pan
pear
penguin
pie
puzzle

PAGE 33
Qq
quail
quarter
queen
question
quilt

PAGE 34
Rr
rabbit
rain
ring
robe
rocket

PAGE 35
Rr
raccoon
rake
robot
rug
rope

PAGE 36
Ss
sandwich
seal
sink
soup
sock

PAGE 37
Ss
saw
seven
scissors
soap
sun

PAGE 38
Tt
taco
table
tie
tooth
turkey

PAGE 39
Tt
tent
tiger
toe
tub
turtle

PAGE 40
Uu
umbrella
umpire
under
underwear
up

PAGE 41
Vv
van
vase
vest
vine
volcano

PAGE 42
Ww
wagon
web
wig
window
worm

PAGE 43
Xx
ax
box
fox
mix
six

PAGE 44
Yy
yam
yard
yarn
yawn
yo-yo

PAGE 45
Zz
zebra
zero
zigzag
zipper
zoo

Note: Picture words are listed in the order they appear, clockwise, starting at the left.

Lift-the-Flap Alphabet • © 2011 by Betty Jo Evers • Scholastic Teaching Resources